A VAUGHAN WILLIAMS

ORGAN ALBUM

T0346867

OXFORD UNIVERSITY PRESS
MUSIC DEPARTMENT GREAT CLARENDON STREET OXFORD OX2 6DP

CONTENTS

1. A WEDDING TUNE FOR ANN

Edited by CHRISTOPHER MORRIS

R. VAUGHAN WILLIAMS

This piece was written for the wedding of Miss Ann Pain on 27 October 1943. The original is on two staves, with no indications of pedals and changes of manuals. The tempo markings, dynamics, and slurs are the composer's.

© Oxford University Press 1964
OXFORD UNIVERSITY PRESS, MUSIC DEPARTMENT, GREAT CLARENDON STREET, OXFORD OX2 6DP
Photocopying this copyright material is ILLEGAL.

2. GREENSLEEVES

Arranged by
STANLEY ROPER

Adapted from an Old Air
by
R. VAUGHAN WILLIAMS

Sw. Soft flutes (8 and 4ft.)
Ch. (or Gt.) Gamba 8ft.
Ped. 8ft. Cp. Sw.

This arrangement is on sale as a separate publication

© Oxford University Press, 1947
A Vaughan Williams Album for Organ

A Vaughan Williams Album for Organ

A Vaughan Williams Album for Organ

A Vaughan Williams Album for Organ

3. TOCCATA
'ST. DAVID'S DAY'

R. VAUGHAN WILLIAMS

Originally published as No. 2 of *Two Organ Preludes founded on Welsh Folk Songs.*

© Oxford University Press, 1956
A Vaughan Williams Album for Organ

8

A Vaughan Williams Album for Organ

A Vaughan Williams Album for Organ

4. CAROL

Arranged by
HERBERT SUMSION

R. VAUGHAN WILLIAMS

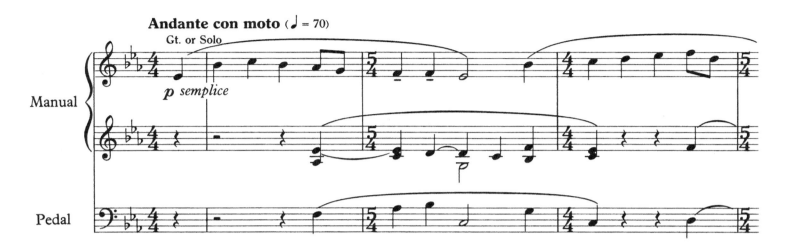

© Oxford University Press, 1938
A Vaughan Williams Album for Organ

A Vaughan Williams Album for Organ

5. ROMANZA
'THE WHITE ROCK'

R. VAUGHAN WILLIAMS

Originally published as No. 1 of *Two Organ Preludes founded on Welsh Folk Songs.*

© Oxford University Press, 1956
A Vaughan Williams Album for Organ

6. PRELUDE
'THE NEW COMMONWEALTH'

Arranged by CHRISTOPHER MORRIS

R. VAUGHAN WILLIAMS

The suggested registration is for a two-manual instrument.
This music has been taken from the film 'The 49th Parallel.'

© Oxford University Press, 1960
A Vaughan Williams Album for Organ

A Vaughan Williams Album for Organ

7. MUSETTE

Arranged by HERBERT SUMSION

R. VAUGHAN WILLIAMS

Ⓒ Oxford University Press, 1938
A Vaughan Williams Album for Organ

A Vaughan Williams Album for Organ

Poco animato

8. LAND OF OUR BIRTH

Arranged by
STAINTON DE B. TAYLOR

R. VAUGHAN WILLIAMS

Prepare:
Solo—Tuba
Swell—Salicional & Gedact 8'
Choir—Clarinet or other solo stop
Great—Diapasons 8'
Pedal—No stops (or quiet 8')
Swell to Pedal
Swell to Great

In the absence of the solo manual, the Tuba solo may be played on a Choir Trumpet; or, on a two-manual instrument, either on a Great reed with full swell accompaniment, or on Swell Trumpet with a less Great to accompany. If there is no pedal reed, the pedal solo passage may be played with Swell reeds coupled to full pedal: the Swell to Great coupler being withdrawn until the change of key.

This music comes from the cantata *Song of Thanksgiving* (O.U.P.)

© Oxford University Press 1961
A Vaughan Williams Album for Organ

A Vaughan Williams Album for Organ

OXFORD UNIVERSITY PRESS